This Is a Let's-Read-and-Find-Out Science Book®

Revised Edition

THE SUN
Our Nearest Star

by Franklyn M. Branley
illustrated by Don Madden

Thomas Y. Crowell   New York

The *Let's-Read-and-Find-Out Science Book* series was originated by Dr. Franklyn M. Branley, Astronomer Emeritus and former Chairman of the American Museum–Hayden Planetarium, and was formerly co-edited by him and Dr. Roma Gans, Professor Emeritus of Childhood Education, Teachers College, Columbia University. For a complete catalog of Let's-Read-and-Find-Out Science Books, write to Thomas Y. Crowell Junior Books, Harper & Row, Publishers, Inc., 10 East 53rd Street, New York, NY 10022.

The Sun: Our Nearest Star.

Text copyright © 1961, 1988 by Franklyn M. Branley
Illustrations copyright © 1988 by Don Madden
All rights reserved. No part of this book may be used or reproduced in any manner whatsoever without written permission except in the case of brief quotations embodied in critical articles and reviews. Printed in the United States of America. For information address Thomas Y. Crowell Junior Books, 10 East 53rd Street, New York, N.Y. 10022. Published simultaneously in Canada by Fitzhenry & Whiteside Limited, Toronto.

Typography by Bettina Rossner
1 2 3 4 5 6 7 8 9 10
Revised Edition

Library of Congress Cataloging-in-Publication Data
Branley, Franklyn Mansfield, 1915–
   The sun: our nearest star.

   (Let's-read-and-find-out science book)
   Summary: Describes the sun and how it provides the light and energy which allow plant and animal life to exist on the Earth.
   1. Sun—Juvenile literature. [1. Sun]
I. Madden, Don, 1927–   ill. II. Title. III. Series.
QB521.5.B7 1988   523.7   87-47764
ISBN 0-690-04680-4
ISBN 0-690-04678-2 (lib. bdg.)

   "A Harper trophy book."
ISBN 0-06-445073-2 (pbk.)   87-45678

THE SUN: Our Nearest Star

At night you can see a lot of stars because the sky is dark.

You can also see a star in daytime, when the sky is bright.
It is the sun. The sun is our daytime star. It is also the star
nearest to us.

The sun is very big. It is much bigger than Earth. The sun is almost a million miles across. If Earth were this little dot, the sun would be this big.

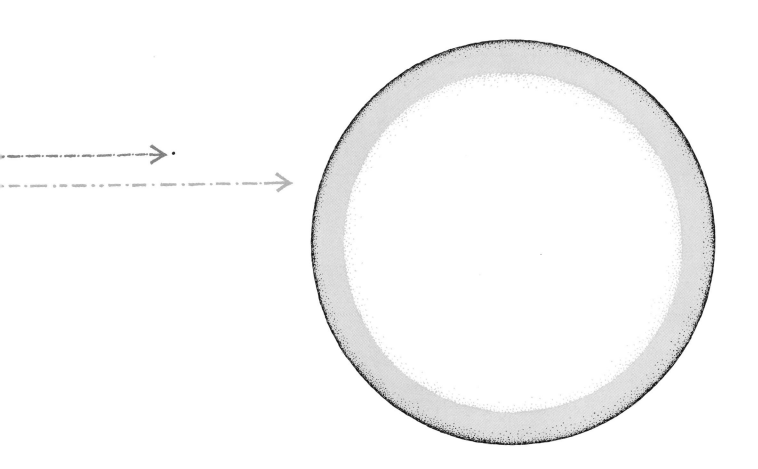

The sun is very far away from Earth. It is much farther from us than the moon. It is 240,000 miles from Earth to the moon. But it is 93,000,000 miles to the sun. Suppose a spaceship went from Earth to the moon and could get there in three days. The same spaceship would take three years to get to the sun.

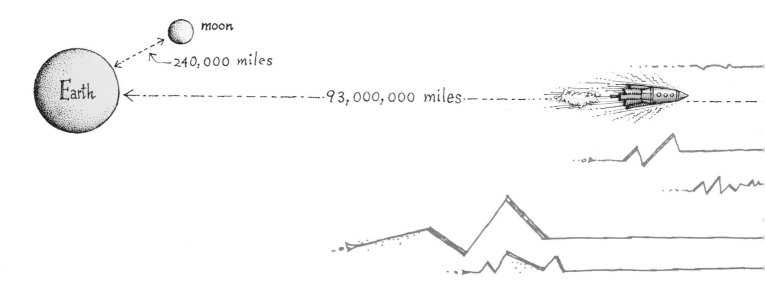

moon

240,000 miles

Earth

93,000,000 miles

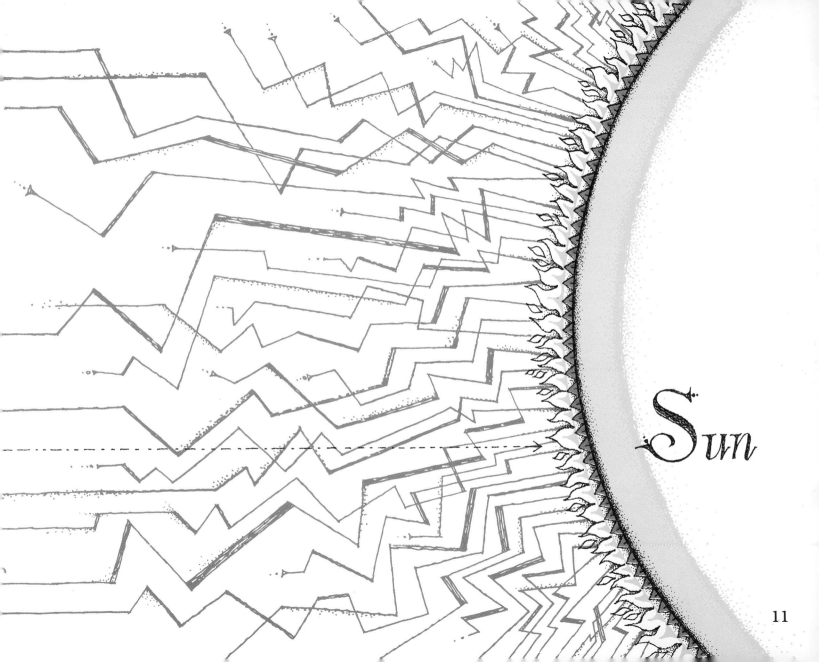

Sun

11

And remember, the sun is our nearest star. All other stars are much farther away from us. It takes eight minutes for light to travel from the sun to Earth. The next star beyond the sun is so far away that light from it takes over four years to reach us.

The sun is made of hot gases. Most of the sun is hydrogen gas. There are lots of other materials, too, including iron, gold, copper, and tin. They are not solid, as they are on Earth. All of them are gases. They are gases because they are so hot.

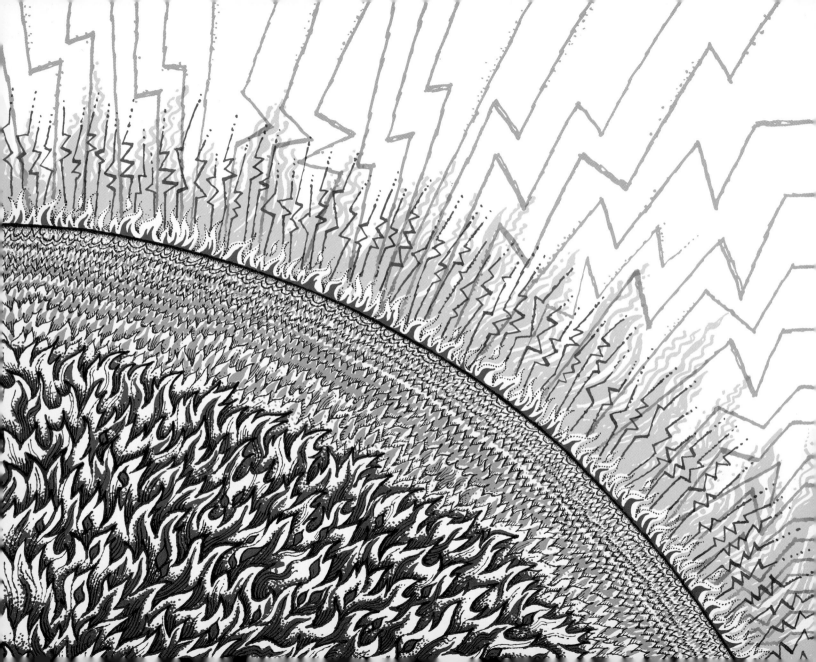

The sun is so hot that a spaceship could never get close to it. If it did, the spaceship would melt. The temperature on the sun's surface is 10,000 degrees Fahrenheit.

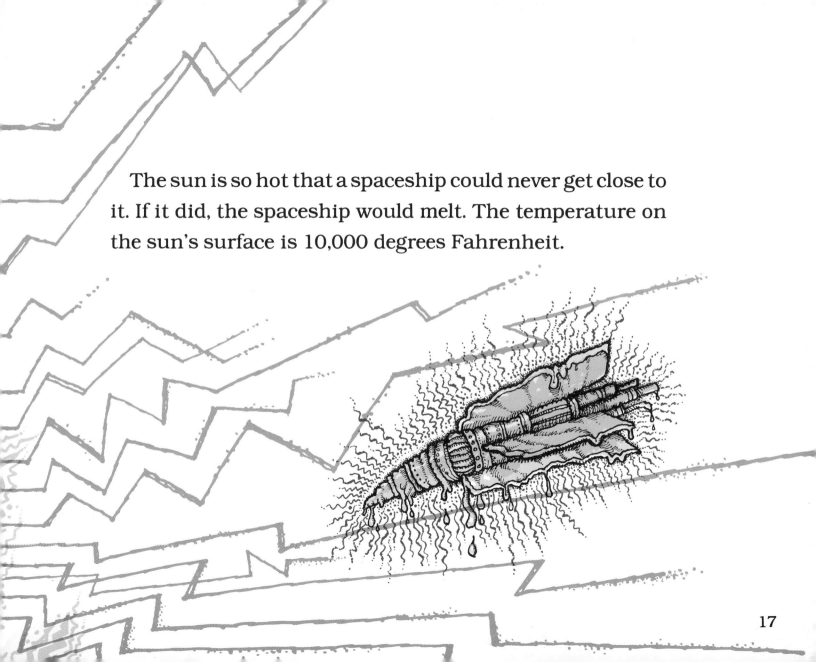

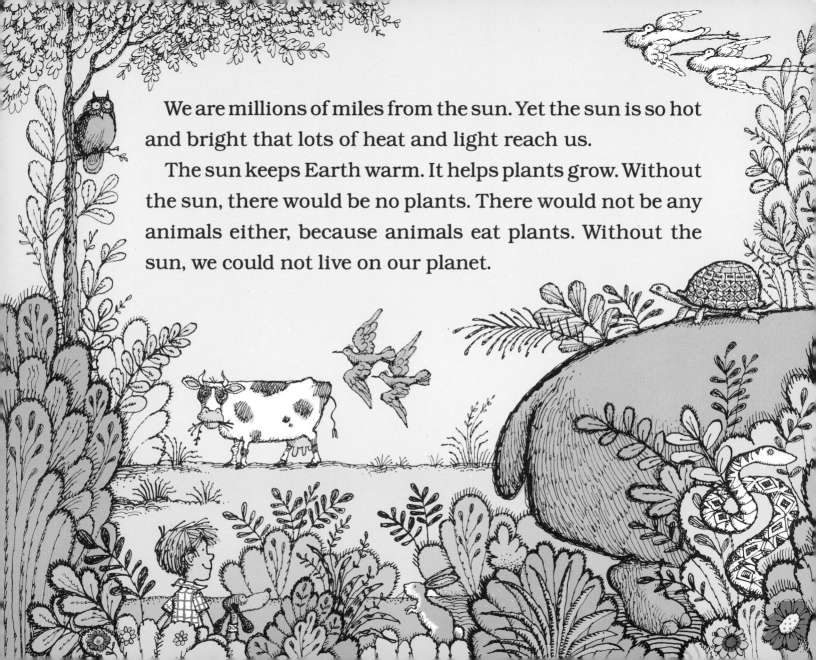

We are millions of miles from the sun. Yet the sun is so hot and bright that lots of heat and light reach us.

The sun keeps Earth warm. It helps plants grow. Without the sun, there would be no plants. There would not be any animals either, because animals eat plants. Without the sun, we could not live on our planet.

You can do an experiment to prove that the sun helps things grow.

Put some soil into two paper cups. Plant four beans in each cup. Cover the beans with a bit of soil.

21

Put one cup in a sunny spot, and the other in a dark place. Water the soil. Put only a little water in each cup, just enough to make the soil damp.

After about a week the beans will start to sprout. Those in the sunlight will grow well. At first those in the dark will also grow well.

Water the sprouts for three or four weeks, or even longer. A spoonful of water every four days or so is enough. Watch for differences between the plants in the sun and those in the dark.

You will discover that your beans need the sun to keep growing. All plants do, and animals too.

The sun helps plants and animals grow.

It also gives us energy. Most of the energy we use on Earth comes from the sun. Energy from the sun is called solar energy.

Energy from the sun can be trapped to heat water and to heat houses.

27

Even the energy in coal, oil, and gasoline, which is made from oil, comes from the sun.

Millions of years ago the sun's energy helped plants and animals grow. When the plants and animals died, they were packed together and changed to coal and oil. So coal and oil are really stored-up solar energy.

Millions of years ago the sun warmed our planet. It keeps us warm today. The sun will still be shining millions of years from now. Of all the stars in the sky, the sun, our daytime star, is by far the most important one for you and me.